THEN & NOW

BROOKVILLE

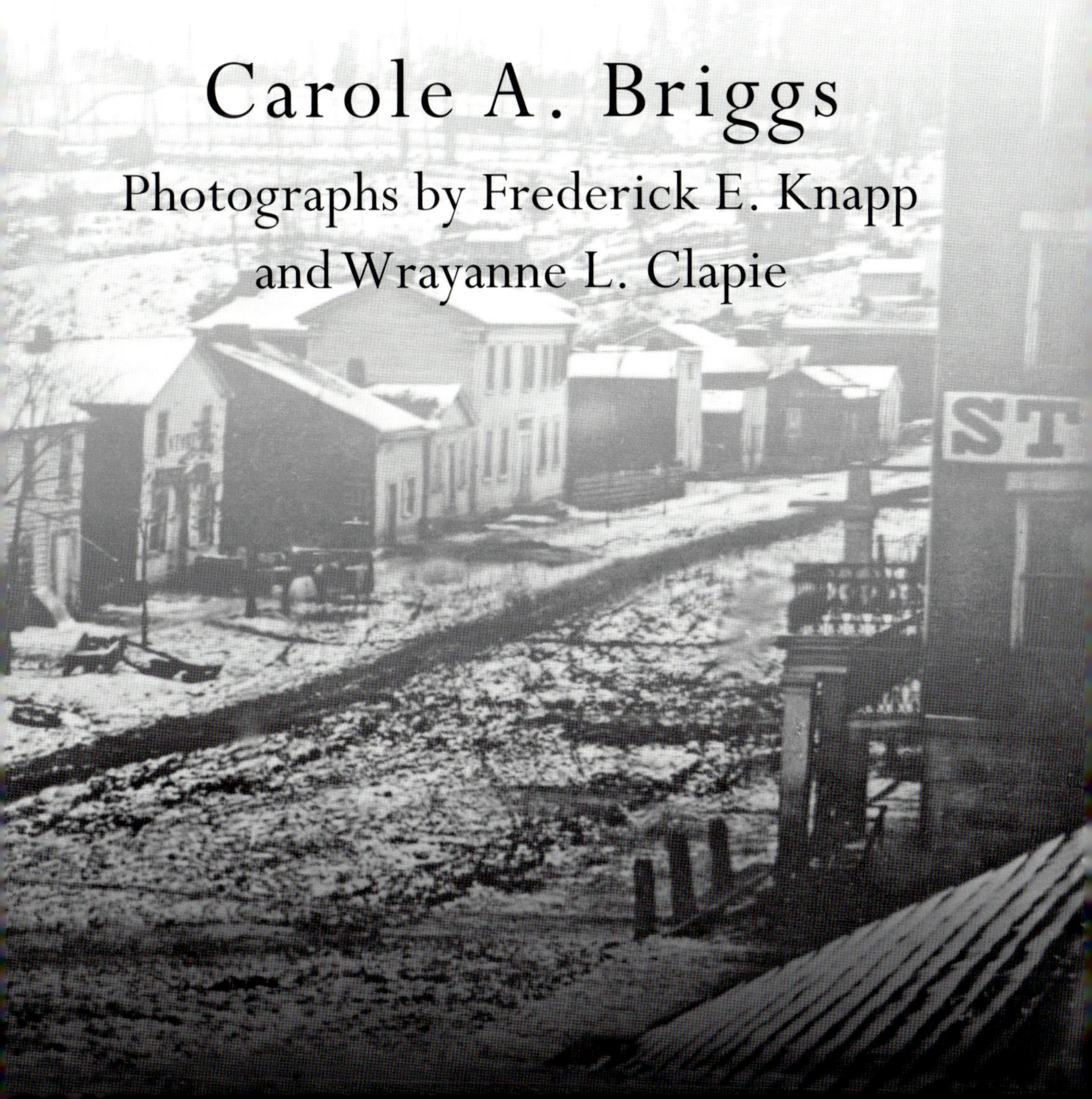

Carole A. Briggs

Photographs by Frederick E. Knapp and Wrayanne L. Clapie

ISBN 978-0-7385-7374-8

Library of Congress Control Number: 2010925882

Published by Arcadia Publishing
Charleston, South Carolina

Printed in the United States of America

For all general information, please contact Arcadia Publishing:
Telephone 843-853-2070
Fax 843-853-0044
E-mail sales@arcadiapublishing.com
For customer service and orders:
Toll-Free 1-888-313-2665

Visit us on the Internet at www.arcadiapublishing.com

On the Front Cover: In 1923, proud Civil War veterans gathered near Harrison Matson's building to rededicate the monument that now included their fallen comrades and the names of World War I veterans. Today parts of the monument have been incorporated into new monuments on the courthouse lawn, and Matson's building is occupied by a variety of businesses. (Then image courtesy JCHS Collection; now image courtesy Wrayanne L. Clapie.)

On the Back Cover: An ambitious project of Brookville leaders, the Brookville Park Auditorium building became known as the "White Elephant" when plans for its completion were overwhelmed by World War I and the Great Depression. (Courtesy JCHS Collection.)

Contents

Acknowledgments

We are grateful for the interest that has led to this volume of selected photographs by Brookville photographer Frederick E. Knapp.

Knapp opened his studio in 1898. After his death in 1948, much of his life's work was carted to the town dump, but *Jeffersonian Democrat* editor Harry Eugene "Pud" McMurray recognized its worth. He and son Don retrieved many of the glass-plate and film negatives. Hauled up to the second floor of the newspaper office, they remained there for many years.

Historic Brookville, Inc. (HBI) was created in 1982, and two years later a 90-acre area was designated a National Register Historic District. Meanwhile, amateur photographer Don Snyder retired to the community, and, with Don McMurray's approval, made first-generation prints from the original negatives before returning them to their storage spot.

When the Jefferson County Historical Society (JCHS) built a small archive in 1993, HBI began discussions with the board about the long-term preservation of the Knapp Collection. The two organizations created the Brookville Heritage Trust, with the JCHS assuming responsibility for their preservation. A Pennsylvania Historical and Museum Commission grant funded appropriate conservation materials, as well as the creation of 35-mm negatives and a new set of first-generation images. Later volunteer archivist Jennifer Landry digitized and catalogued the more than 550 images into the PastPerfect Software database. Today as additional film and glass-plate negatives continue to surface, they are added to the Knapp Collection.

When teacher Wrayanne Clapie expressed interest in working with the JCHS on a photography project, a grant from the Elk County Council on the Arts (the regional arts-funding partnership supported by the Pennsylvania Council on the Arts) made it possible for her to revisit and photograph the sites Knapp had photographed between 1898 and 1945. "Then & Now: Photographs of Frederick E. Knapp and Wrayanne Clapie" proved to be a popular exhibit with both county residents and visitors from beyond.

This book will continue the comparison long after the exhibit. We are grateful to reviewers Randon Bartley, William McCracken, Kathy Smith, and David Taylor, who contributed their expertise and knowledge of Brookville to this project, and to Biandi Photography and Art for assistance with scanning.

Finally, Joellyn McIlvaine and Luann Harkens, granddaughters of Frederick E. Knapp, along with Norma Jean Ford Ross, a distant relative, have graciously provided funding for expenses incurred in both the exhibit and this publication.

Unless noted otherwise, all *then* photographs are those of Frederick E. Knapp, and *now* photographs are the work of Wrayanne Clapie.

Introduction

Nestled in the valley where the Sandy Lick and North Fork meet to form Red Bank Creek, where Native Americans once grew maize, and where hills rise in every direction, lays Brookville, the seat of Jefferson County, Pennsylvania. Early maps describe this area of western Pennsylvania as the "Buffalo Swamp" and the place of the "People of Unknown Origin."

Most Native Americans were gone when settlers with European and African roots arrived intent upon timbering and farming. Joseph Barnett, his brother Andrew, and his wife's brother Samuel Scott had arrived about 1795, and with the help of nine Native Americans they built a mill on Mill Creek at a place now called Port Barnett. Then Joseph left, returning two years later with his family. Less than a decade later, in 1804, the legislature carved Jefferson County out of Lycoming County. It included much of what is known today as Forest, Elk, and Jefferson Counties.

Other settlers then arrived. One was Moses Knapp, who built his mill at the confluence of the rivers, becoming the first settler of European origin to reside within the present borough limits. Three commissioners appointed by the legislature designated Brookville the county seat in 1830, and surveyors laid out the town in a grid pattern, with most lots measuring 58 feet by 150 feet. Lots were sold for $30 to $300, and specific ones were reserved for public buildings and a burial ground. But Brookville grew slowly. Roads into the area, like the Susquehanna and Waterford toll road completed in 1822, were primitive. Trees were tall, and larger towns were far away.

Nevertheless, people did arrive, including fugitive slaves from the south. In 1861, Jefferson County men answered the call of Pres. Abraham Lincoln and fought in the 105th, 67th, 135th, 148th, 206th, 211th, and other units, leaving their womenfolk to pick up the plow and maintain the home front.

Men timbered and families farmed. Two local innovations made growth in the lumber trade possible: the bracket dam system for creating artificial flooding on the shallow river systems, and the logging railroad built by Wright and Pier in 1864. Raftsmen constructed large rafts of timber or sawn boards, and the high-water seasons in the spring and fall saw them plying the waters between the small town and major lumber markets downstream like Pittsburgh. Logging railroads made it possible to move logs longer distances to the rivers. Families whose fortunes were made in lumbering built many of the fine older homes and commercial buildings that may be seen today.

Then, within the decade that followed the Civil War, the Low Grade Division of the Allegheny Valley Railroad traversed the county. Now timber, coal, and other natural resources could be marketed in exchange for products desired by the rising entrepreneurs and their families.

Two years later, in 1876, the last of the four "big fires" occurred, burning substantial numbers of the wooden buildings in the Main Street section. These were replaced by brick structures that, today, are pristine examples of late-19th century residential and commercial architecture. The largest include the Jefferson County Courthouse (1869), the Parker P. Blood building (1875), the Nathan Greene Edelblute building (1850 and 1875), and the Marlin Opera House (1883).

Brookville had a number of diverse industries: a ladder factory, two breweries, a number of hotels, furniture and glass factories, several livery stables, carriage manufacturers, a woolen mill, and foundries. An axe factory produced 250 axes per day, and the Twyford Motor Company, which operated around 1905, produced at least six of the world's first four-wheel-drive automobiles. Then new technologies developed, and these industries disappeared.

Coal production declined at the end of World War I, and the county's economic growth waned. Like many families across the country, Jefferson County families endured the Great Depression. Then, when the Sylvania Company opened a plant to manufacture vacuum tubes during World War II, more than 1,000 people went to work. The company moved out in 1964, resulting in a recessed economy.

Born in 1869, photographer Frederick E. Knapp witnessed these changes and recorded many with his camera. He was the great-grandson of Moses Knapp, the first Brookville settler of European ancestry. Raised on a Pine Creek Township farm and educated in Brookville, Knapp worked on the family farm and did some stone masonry before becoming an apprentice with Brookville photographer E. C. Hall. He further crafted his skills in Pittsburgh before returning to Brookville in 1898, when he bought the studio of J. S. Vasbinder.

By 1917, historian William J. McKnight could write that Knapp had "a reputation of being a high-class exponent of the art" of photography. He was also an involved community member and Methodist layman.

When Knapp died on March 2, 1948, timbering, which had diminished significantly by 1900, was on its way back as a major industry. This time, though, the product was hardwood, like black cherry, not pine and hemlock. During the next three decades, schools consolidated, banks merged, neighboring communities built malls, and the federal government constructed Interstate 80 north of Brookville. Retail stores closed. The American Hotel was demolished. Gas stations and motels opened on "the strip."

In 1984, Brookville's downtown and adjacent residential areas were named a National Register Historic District and became one of Pennsylvania's first Main Street Projects. Since then, significant dollars have been invested in the preservation and restoration of buildings in the Historic District. A gateway to Cook Forest, Clear Creek State Park, and the Allegheny National Forest and part of the Pennsylvania Wilds and the Lumber Heritage Region of the Commonwealth, Historic Brookville welcomes many visitors each year.

CHAPTER 1

Historic Brookville

Photographers appeared in Brookville before the Civil War, and one of them climbed the steps of the courthouse to set up his view camera and record Main Street. Looking west are properties owned by Hall, McClain, Dickey, Bishop, and Henderson. In 1984, ninety acres encompassing nearly 300 buildings constructed between 1830 and 1930 were designated as a National Register Historic District. (Courtesy JCHS Collection.)

Commissioners located and named Brookville the seat of Jefferson County in 1830. Builders completed the jail first, then the first courthouse. County business moved to the Presbyterian church when the present courthouse underwent construction in 1867. Costing $86,413, its proportions, particularly the cupola or bell tower, are classically derived and formal. Electricity arrived in 1897, inspiring Amelia Clark and the Village Improvement Society to raise funds and dedicate the lighted drinking fountain in 1903.

During Prohibition, Sheriff Milo Milford's department led raids throughout the county and then stored illegal stills and gambling machines in a basement room before disposal. After the 1933 repeal of Prohibition, the room became the assessor's office, and as county business increased, other nooks and crannies were put to use. In the 1970s, the old county home north of Brookville was turned into office space. In 1993, many county offices were relocated to Jefferson Place, a new building on Main Street.

During his term, President Judge Charles Corbet (1916–1926) recognized that the courthouse needed repair and county business required more space, but it was not until the term of President Judge William Darr (1926–1936) that construction got underway. This time, county business moved to the "White Elephant," or the Brookville Park Auditorium building, while the new wing was built. Architectural details blend in with the original building. In 2009, the courthouse was renovated again.

During his term, Judge Edwin Snyder (1972–1992) recommended refurbishing the main courtroom. The project was completed in 1998 and included a new and expanded jury box, refurbished wall sconces, freshly painted walls with a marble-like finish, gold-leaf ceiling overlays, hanging light fixtures, a new sound system, and new carpeting. In his remarks at the dedication, Pennsylvania's Chief Justice John P. Flaherty said, "This could very well be the most beautiful courtroom in Pennsylvania. . . . It is very inspiring."

Civil War veterans are posing here before the monument rededicated to World War I veterans on "All Soldiers' Day" on July 1, 1923. The memorial, with a fourth and new bronze tablet listing additional names, was first dedicated in 1919. Robert Barr, who also built the original courthouse, the academy, and several other early brick structures, built the Harrison Matson building (1849) that is behind them. Parts of the monument were incorporated into new monuments when the courthouse lawn was redesigned.

People once socialized within their neighborhoods, churches, and secret societies like the Masons, Knights of Pythias, and Independent Order of Odd Fellows (IOOF). The IOOF maintained rooms above the dry goods stores of Burton and Cooley and D. A. Henderson in the Parker Blood building. Later the home of Wein's Department Store and the telephone company, the building houses the Area Agency on Aging, Penn State Cooperative Extension offices, and the District Justice Office today.

Dry goods clerk Nathan Greene Edelblute married Rosetta Frank in 1860. His business grew, and by 1875 he also was raising trotters on land between the rivers and racing them throughout the northeast. When the "big fire" of 1874 burned his neighbor's building to the ground, he bought the land and built a new dry goods store for himself and a millinery shop for Rosetta's sister. In 2004, Nathan's building became home to the Jefferson County History Center.

The horse-drawn cart and bricked street indicate an early Knapp photograph taken from Main Street's east end. Today the familiar roofline of the Baptist parsonage and the curved steps of the Midwifery Service are apparent (left), as are the courthouse cupola, Parker Blood building, and History Center (right). Brookville's Main Street project included the restoration of many retail and residential facades and the addition of awnings, brick, and concrete sidewalks, period electric street lighting, and tree plantings.

Some say Brookville is the smallest community east of the Mississippi River to have a full-service YMCA. Organized sometime before 1905, plans for a new building were underway when Mechanic's Hall burned in June 1915. Citizens responded to a whirlwind campaign that raised $41,158 in a week's time; the present building, designed by DuBois architects Harrington and Howard, opened in 1917. Renovated several times, the building includes a pool, showers, dining room, gym, exercise rooms, classrooms, and offices.

Water safety was an early concern for the community. Before the present building opened in 1916, the YMCA staff offered lessons at North Fork Park. The inclusion of a pool in the new building and swimming lessons alleviated worries about people drowning even more. Today swimming classes are available at the Hickory Grove Elementary School pool. The YMCA pool is still used for lessons, and a full program of water exercises and activities is available for adults as well. (Then image courtesy Brookville Area YMCA.)

The YMCA gym has been the scene of basketball tournaments, organization meetings, dances, craft shows, and dinners. Today people of all ages use the building's facilities to exercise, play games, swim, use computers, and attend classes. The YMCA offers a wide variety of children's programs, including before- and after-school care, the PAL Nursery School, day camps for preschoolers and students, play groups, and classes, including dance and golf.

John Matson arrived to timber in 1805. His son, Uriah, also timbered and built this three-story building in 1858. Many businesses have come and gone: Loebman's, Matson Bros. Groceries, the L. A. Leathers Department Store, McCrory's, Wolf Furniture, Kessler's Furniture, and Jode's Fashions. Now home to the offices of owner Paul Gray, the upper floors have seen many tenants, including one Frederick Knapp, who had his studio on the second floor from the 1920s to his retirement in 1945.

Moving west from Uriah Matson's building are McKnight and Son Drug Store (1871), White Hall, Brookville Title and Trust (1876), National Bank of Brookville, and the Marlin Opera House block (1885). Following the Civil War, Col. Silas J. Marlin entered the lumber business and, by 1883, had begun building the Italianate commercial building. His large building is home now to Medi-Home Health Care, McCabe Drugstore, Brookville Flower Shop, Jefferson County Home Makers, Randy's Electronics, and second-floor tenants.

The Marlin Opera House on the second floor of the Marlin Opera House building seated 900. The setting for live entertainment and graduations between 1884 and 1902, people went elsewhere for entertainment when the nickelodeon and movies arrived in town. The seats are gone, but gaslights and wall stencils remain. Relatively unchanged for nearly a century, PBS used this "incredible artifact of American theater history" as one of the settings for a Stephen Foster documentary in 1999.

Ben Craig's drugstore occupied one of six retail spaces on the first floor of the Marlin Opera House building. For more than 30 years, he dispensed sundaes, sodas, and 11 flavors of ice cream over the marble counter. Flavors included claret, sarsaparilla, and ginger, and if one counts the tins of Horlick's Malted Milk Powder atop the ornate soda fountain, chocolate malts also must have been a popular treat. McCabe Drug Store occupies the space today.

The banner proclaiming Dr. Babcock and Halls' Photography dates this photograph as one of Knapp's earliest, yet some familiar rooflines remain. Looking west on Main Street from Diamond Alley, structures include the Rodgers-Canning Building (Goodwill), a law office (Farmers National Bank), Plyler Grocery (Dittman Consignment), the Arthurs' home (offices of McKinley and Company), (the next four have been replaced by Dollar General and the J. W. DeMotte Building), the Henderson's home (offices of Dennison, Dennison and Harper), and the tin shop (DeMans).

Knapp had studios in at least three Main Street buildings. Returning from Pittsburgh in 1898, he bought the photography business of J. S. Vasbinder, located where Farmers National Bank is today. This early and snowy photograph, looking east from present-day DeMans, shows his second studio. Recognizable rooflines are Goodwill, Farmers National Bank, Dittman Consignment, and McKinley and Company. The other buildings, including Knapp's studio, have been replaced by Dollar General and the J. W. DeMotte building.

The lumbermen, salesmen, and other travelers who arrived by stagecoach and, after 1874, by train stayed in one of the many hotels on Main Street. Built just west of the courthouse in 1845, the original American Hotel burned in 1856 and was rebuilt the next year. It served the community more than a century before being razed in 1963 and replaced by a gas station. The current owner, Historic Brookville, Inc., plans to replace it with a small park.

The American Hotel was large. Sterk's News Stand and the hotel dining room adjoined the lobby. Over the building's lifetime, the American Café, a shoe shine stand, Western Union, a barber, a billiard room, and a pay telephone station occupied first floor space; successively, Heasley and Reitz, Barrett and Reitz Clothing, and Reitz's occupied a first floor retail space. In the rear, a livery and barn housed horses and hacks. Census records list several permanent residents, maids, clerks, and laundresses living there.

The large redbrick Central Hotel, diagonal from the courthouse, replaced the Franklin House. Constructed in 1876, the three-story building had retail space on the first floor with rooms above and more retail space on the lower level. The Lakes-to-Sea Restaurant operated on the corner during the 1920s and 1930s, and Rubin's Department Store replaced Weiss Brothers Dry Goods (1917–1947). Current tenants include attorney Sharon Smith, It's a Dollar, and Miller's Precious Treasures.

An early Brookville hotel, the Globe (below), had a succession of owners between 1830 and 1857 when a new owner, C. N. Kretz, renamed it the Jefferson House. Magnus Allgeier and L. L. Reitz bought it in 1883. Signs painted on the windows highlighted the bar room. Philip Allgeier replaced the original building in 1904 and operated the New Jefferson Hotel until 1918. In 1882, John and Amelia Henderson, a milliner, purchased the building to the left, which was constructed by Robert Barr.

Pittsburgh architect Harry S. Bair added the rear theater addition and replaced the two-story portico with a marquee. Named the Columbia, *Ripley's Believe It Or Not* highlighted its unique screen placement at the front. Silent and talking pictures were popular there until television arrived in the mid-1950s. The Scarlet Cord Teen Center and Dead Center Arms occupy the building today. Amelia Henderson's millinery shop to the left now houses the Pennsylvania State Liquor Store and Brookville Heritage Suites, a bed-and-breakfast.

The Clements House occupied this site almost from Brookville's founding to the "big fire" of 1871, when it burned to the ground. The new Commercial Hotel replaced it. Acquired by the American Hotel, then in 1921 by Brookville Title and Trust, the first floor was converted to a bank, and the upper floor rooms were leased to the American Hotel. Today the Old Hat resale shop and the courthouse are the only 19th-century buildings that remain on this block.

CHAPTER 2

BUSINESS AND INDUSTRY

Early in his career, Knapp photographed the remnants of the once vibrant timber industry that had filled the valley—the squared timbers of Litch's bracket dam along the North Fork and the tracks of Matson and Heidrick's logging railroad in the foreground. The area east of the river once belonged to mill owner Thomas K. Litch.

Litch's mill, later owned by Richard McConnell Matson and Levi Heidrick and finally by A. W. Cook, was demolished in 1911. During the 1920s, the Brookville Motor Company began selling Fords, Lincolns, and Fordson tractors in this building. Easily recognizable are the cut stone wall ascending the hill and the rear of the home and offices at 100 Franklin, situated at the end of Main Street. Ben Craig's dark, four-storied home has been replaced by maturing oak trees.

By the 1930s, a new building and a new car dealership had replaced the Brookville Motor Company. The end of the Dixie Diner, one of two diners in town then, is visible to the left of the Brookville Chevrolet Company. Known over the years as Fulton Chevrolet, then Gromley Chevrolet, both sides of East Main Street are now the lot of the latest car dealership on the property, Brookville Chevrolet Pontiac Buick Cadillac, Inc.

L. A. Leathers arrived in Brookville in 1901 at age 21 to begin half a century in business. His early success with a department store led to the first Ford dealership in the area in 1910. It was located on Madison Street. The building was razed to make room for the new quarters of the Brookville Volunteer Fire Department (BVFD) that was dedicated in 1994. In 2009, the BVFD celebrated 100 years of service to the community.

Knapp's studio occupied this area prior to John R. Baker's construction of this 1919 building. L. A. Leathers purchased the Baker Buick Company facility in 1923. He named his firm the Lakes-to-Sea Motor Company after the newly paved highway and displayed, sold, and serviced automobiles for more than 20 years. The A&P occupied it between World War II and the 1960s. Now owned by J. W. DeMotte Real Estate, Dollar General occupies the first floor and DeMans Team Sports the second.

Automobiles require service. Automobiles need gas. As horse-drawn wagons and buggies disappeared and liveries closed, automobile service garages opened, and gasoline pumps appeared near curbs. A. M. Reitz named his garage on South White Street the Dodge Brothers. Sam Strano has tuned up and repaired automobiles in the same building since the early 1970s, but he works on foreign imports, not Model Ts or Dodges, and he orders parts on the Internet.

In 1929, Walter J. Sandt built the Auto Service Station where attendants changed tires, pumped Pennzoil gas, washed windshields, and provided all the services needed to keep cars running. An example of roadside architecture, DuBois architect Russell Howard designed the stucco-on-tile building constructed by master builder John Carr. Mrs. Sandt, who thought the tower "too plain," suggested the perched china doves. Originally there were three. Today the building includes medical offices and the West Penn Motor Club.

At the start of the 20th century, industry flourished in Brookville, and agriculture flourished around it. Farmers tilled their fields in the spring, made hay on sunny summer days, and harvested crops in the fall. Pictured near the center of these photographs, the French Second Empire residence with the mansard roof on Western Avenue named Woodland Home was the successive residence of R. D. Taylor, C. M. Carrier, and Amor Deemer. It remains a private home today.

Timber and coal created substantial wealth for Brookville between 1865 and 1917. That wealth was invested in factories producing ladders, axes, furniture, glass, carriages, and wool and foundries producing mining trams and locomotives. Many of these factories, like the Hercules Manufacturing Factory, were situated in the southeast section of the community. Today aluminum ladders are manufactured in places like China; and groups, like the Brookville Community Theater, use the building (above and now owned by Paul Gray) for storage.

August Boulanger brought a group of Belgian glassworkers to Brookville in 1901 to work in the new Brookville Glass and Tile Factory, one of many glass factories that stretched in a large swath from West Virginia to New York State. Workers produced window glass and lived in the area called "Belgiumtown." A lawsuit over patents, labor problems, taxes, and conversion expenses caused the company to foreclose in 1924. The building was razed in 1963.

Early woodworkers in Brookville made just about everything people needed, from cradles to caskets, in their small shops. Between the 1890s and 1943, the A. D. Deemer Furniture Company, located in southeast Brookville, produced and marketed a large line of oak and maple furniture that included tables, cupboards, wardrobes, dry sinks, washstands, dressers, bedsteads, and cradles. Imitation walnut and mahogany finishes also were available. The business survived four fires. Matson Lumber is the present owner.

The first automobile with four-wheel drive and power steering was developed and built in the Twyford Motorcar Factory in Brookville. The best estimate is that six models were produced before the company foreclosed and Robert Twyford moved to Texas. Then the building became the Union Auto Specialties Company, Humphrey Machine Shop, and the Leon Jordan Machine Shop, respectively, before being torn down in 1974. A Twyford replica, built by William McCracken, is exhibited at the Jefferson County History Center.

Industry prospered along the Red Bank. Brookville Manufacturing Company workers built wagons; nearby Michael Murphy built buggies. Both buildings burned in a spectacular fire in 1932. The Plato warehouse (below left), the Belvedere Opera House (below right), and the tower and flag of the Central School building high on "Knowledge Knob" are no longer there, but the distinctive rooftop of the building owned by Sarveys and housing McLean Publishing, at 301 Main Street, is in the center left of both photographs.

In a shop on the south side of Red Bank Creek, Charles Albert Bowdish and his brothers built truck bodies, and each Christmas between 1919 and 1955 Charles created an exhibit in his nearby home. Thousands came to see it. His exhibit has evolved into Pittsburgh's Miniature Railroad and Village™ and the Jefferson County History Center's Bowdish Exhibit. The building on the right has housed Allgeier's Spring Brewery, Brookville Ice Cream and Dairy, Mason Beverages, and now Plyler Beverage.

Following the YMCA's successful whirlwind campaign, the town fathers decided to try it again and erect an auditorium on land near the rivers. The walls were up and the roof was on when World War I and insufficient funds slowed progress, leading some to call it a "white elephant," a property requiring much care and expense but yielding little profit. In 1926, during the courthouse renovation, before county offices could move in, workers laid pine floors and installed a furnace.

Used for horse stalls, automobile shows, Bowdish Stock Company plays and flower exhibits, and as the temporary courthouse, it was 1943 before the Brookville Park Auditorium building gained a long-term tenant. More than 1,000 workers manufactured vacuum tubes at Sylvania Electric Products, Inc. When the company moved out in 1964, Harold Dinger and two others bought the building and incorporated White-Brook as a custom machine-building shop. Today the company is owned and operated by Dinger's three sons.

The Centennial Building was added to the fairgrounds in 1930, when Brookville celebrated its 1830 founding. People and floats gathered near it after taking part in the centennial parade. The Pickering Street Bridge, a single-span metal truss bridge built in 1905, is seen in the background. The Centennial Building, with a later addition, was also used by Sylvania Electric Products, Inc. between 1943 and 1964 and now is part of White-Brook, Inc.

W. F. Clark witnessed two of Brookville's four big fires, so when he formed a private bank in 1872, it was important that the building be fireproof. He called this small Renaissance Revival building, with black walnut doors and faced with fine-cut stone, the W. F. Clark and Son Bank. Sadly the bank closed when his son became ill in 1879. United Natural Gas had offices there for many years before Sarvey Insurance. Now Ferringer Flowers occupies the building.

"Three banks in a row" included the Jefferson County National Bank (the McKnight building to its left), the Brookville Title and Trust, and the National Bank of Brookville (out of range on the right). In 1927, the Keystone Grocery Store occupied part of the Title and Trust building. The Jefferson County National Bank did not reopen in 1933 after Roosevelt's Bank Holiday. The site of Crooks Clothing for many years, today the 1926 building is home to Hoak Insurance Services.

Brookville Title and Trust, organized in 1903, was the middle of the "three banks in a row" on the south side of Main Street. In 1921, the bank purchased and rebuilt on the Commercial Hotel property, opening in 1922. The American Hotel had rooms on the second floor connected to the hotel itself by an enclosed elevated passage. The passage was removed in 1963, and extensive renovation in 1971 changed the building's height. Today the bank is known as S and T.

An associate judge prior to the Civil War and a delegate to the National Union Convention of 1864, Joseph Henderson built this home for his wife and 11 children in 1877. Upon the death of Mrs. Henderson in 1917, the stately brick building became the offices of attorney Raymond Brown. A line of attorneys followed, including David G. Matson, John Aikman, Donald Dennison, James Dennison, Heidi Ulrich Dennison, and most recently John Dennison (Donald's son) and Troy Harper.

The clothing of the five people posed on the porch at 379 Main Street (below) would indicate Knapp took this photograph prior to World War I, when many families lived in homes on Main Street. Grocer William Shields and his wife, Katherine, lived here with their two sons and daughter. As the county seat, many lawyers have both worked and lived in Brookville. Today the offices of attorneys Achille, Ellermeyer, and Wallisch fill the building.

Many professionals have had offices in the Historic District. Early in the 20th century, the offices of the *Jeffersonian Democrat* were on the south side of this building on Pickering Street, and Dr. Lowry and his assistant cleaned, filled, and pulled teeth on the north side. Later florist Helen Wonderling used the space. Dr. Y. M. Bhatnagar bought the building in 1981 and remodeled it for his gynecological practice. Today the building is vacant.

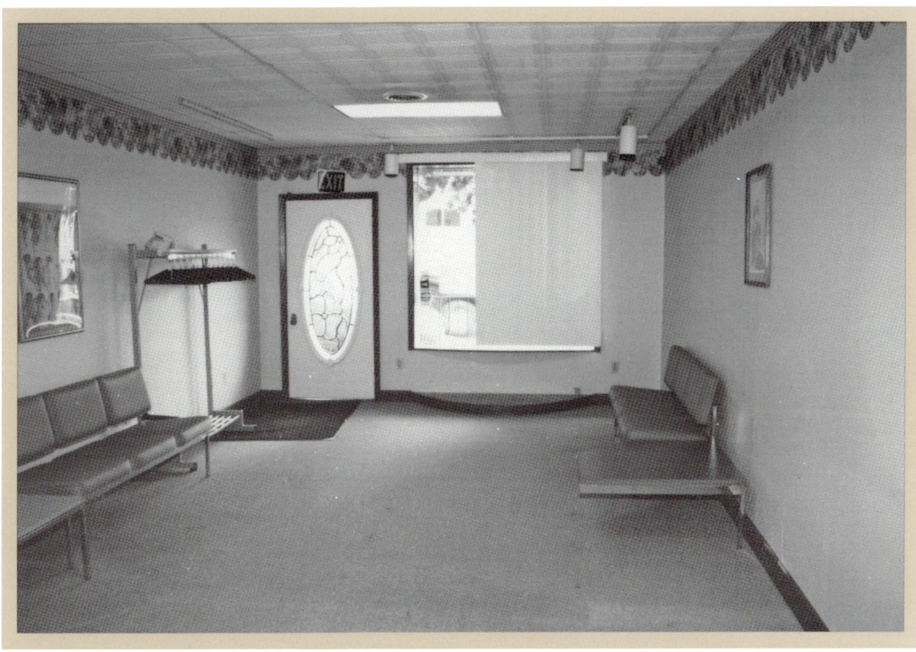

Gilmore and Rufus Reitz moved their furniture, carpet, and undertaking businesses into the commodious space of this building in 1907. Gilmore's brothers, Dick (second to right) and Ralph (right), had met the mule skinner (left) and his mules at the railroad station to accompany them on their way to Broadacres, the farm on State Route 36 north of town. Note the cement horse hitch with the letter "R" along the curb and the E. B. Henderson home to the right.

Knapp photographed this show window in 1929. Later known as R and D Furniture and then Galbraith's R and D Furniture, the store is now known as Galbraith's and displays fine furnishings and carpets in the same window today. Also undertakers, the Reitzs displayed caskets and held viewings on the third floor before moving their undertaking services into the Henderson home in the 1930s. Don Galbraith assumed both businesses in 1963. Today his family operates Galbraith's, and Mark McKinney owns the funeral home.

Matson and Heidrick owned the Litch Mill between 1894 and 1898 before selling it to Cook. Sawyers cut the last log in 1905, and the shrill sound of the mill's whistle no longer punctuated the air. The hills were bare—the timber era was over. People went to work in coal mines, factories, and offices instead. Second-growth timber matured after World War II, and today once again timbering provides a livelihood for many. Cars and SUVs occupy both sides of the street.

When Knapp first began photographing the community, the old Brookville Water Works supplied water to the town. The facility was located on the west side of the North Fork beside the tracks of Matson and Heidrick's logging railroad. By 1911, plans were underway for the new water plant. The old mill came down, and the tracks were removed. What remains the same are the rooflines of several houses on Franklin Avenue.

The North Fork moved timber to market, powered early mills, remains a great recreational resource, and has provided water to homes, businesses, and industry for more than two centuries. Today Interstate 80 soars over the California mission-style water plant built in 1911. In the 1950s, Brookville became the second town in the state to add fluoride to its water in an effort to reduce tooth decay, and in 1990 it earned a top state award for water excellence.

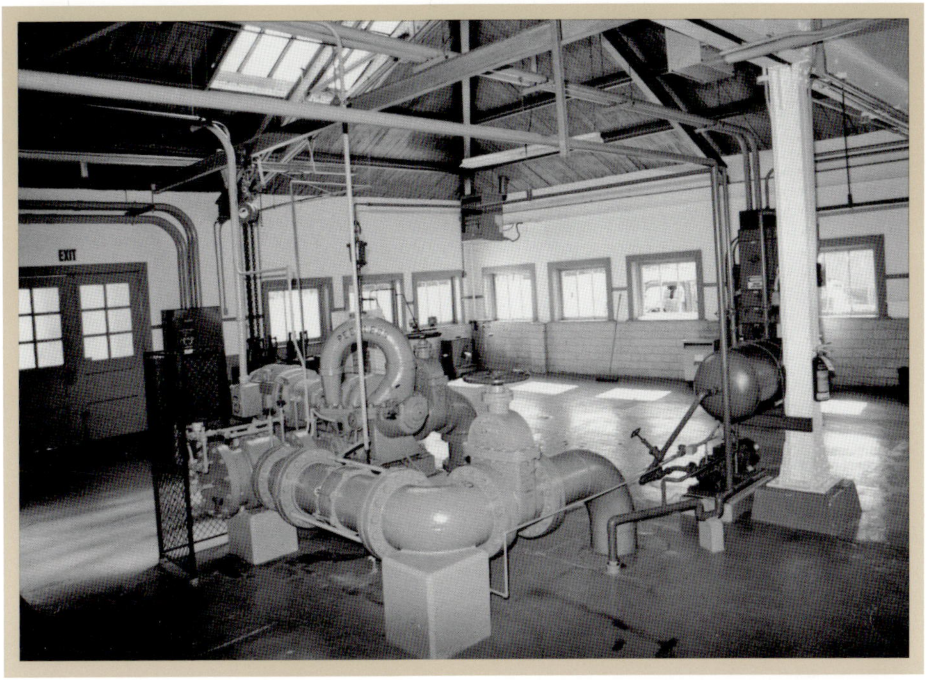

The large 175-horsepower Otto gas engine that pumped water throughout Brookville for many decades is now displayed in the Coolspring Power Museum, just south of Brookville, where one of the foremost collections of early internal combustion technology in the United States is presented in a visitor-friendly manner. Both Brookville Municipal Authority and citizen groups continue to monitor and improve the water quality of the North Fork and its tributaries, and construction has begun on a new water plant.

In 1830, commissioners selected Brookville as the county seat because of its location at the confluence of the North Fork and the Sandy Lick and its centrality in the county. In this image taken from the Church Street hill about a century later, Knapp captured both the spot where his great-great-grandfather built a mill and Brookville's expansion to the east. The Pratt truss bridge and Blake's Hardware Store have been replaced and the Heber Hotel torn down.

CHAPTER 3

RESIDENCES

When Knapp began his career in 1898, horses pulled carriages over brick streets. When he retired in 1945, automobiles rolled along over macadam and concrete. One afternoon, he captured this image of Enoch Loux as he drove his wagon past 10 West Main Street, the home where Fred and his wife, Sydney Wilson, lived with their daughter, Ada Lucille.

A Pennsylvania State Historical Marker identifies the home of Judge Elijah Heath, an outspoken abolitionist who was sued by a Virginia slaveholder and fined for aiding the escape of two fugitive slaves from the old jail in 1834. In 1903, Dr. Charles Matson lived in the house and discovered a secret door and passageway. Archaeological evidence strongly suggests the judge harbored fugitive slaves there. One of the town's oldest residences, his home has undergone considerable change since 1831.

Thomas K. Litch moved from Massachusetts to Pittsburgh before purchasing extensive timber holdings in Jefferson County in 1850 and building a home overlooking the river valley and his lumber mill. His son Edward built this home. Improvements to the house continued before heirs turned it into apartments. Finally abandoned, Frank and Mary Fleeger bought it in 1968, opened an art studio, and began restoration. New owners continued the restoration, and today it is again a private residence. (Then image courtesy JCHS Collection.)

The Greek Revival–pillared residence (1848) of Joseph E. Hall became the home of Samuel B. and Rebecca Arthurs after their marriage. When Rebecca died in 1955, her will stipulated that the building become a library. For two decades, the library located here served the community before the weight of the growing collection made the move to the Hughes Market building necessary. The Arthurs home is listed on the National Register of Historic Places and now is rented.

Dr. A. C. McKinley graduated from medical school in 1908 and returned to Corsica to practice medicine. In 1929, he, his wife, and their seven children moved into this home, previously inhabited by President Judge Elijah Heath Clark. McKinley's four sons, Oscar, Randon, Wayne, and Mark, became doctors, and together the five physicians provided more than 200 years of medical service to the county. The porch is gone, and the building is home to Healthsource Chiropractic and Progressive Rehab now.

Richard McConnell Matson's father and grandfather were timbermen in Jefferson County. "Mac" began a law career but in 1883 was drawn to the lumber business. He and his partner, Levi Heidrick, bought the Litch Mill in 1894 and operated it until selling it to A. W. Cook. During this time, they built a logging railroad to transport timber. Mac built a new home on Main Street in 1903. Later the office of Nationwide Insurance, it is now privately owned.

Between 1885 and 1930, many of the early 19th-century homes built on Jefferson Street, one block north of Main Street, were replaced by bigger American foursquare homes with large porches, bay windows, and third-floor dormers; some had ballrooms on the third floor. In 1930, policeman Fred Smith assisted a parade of automobiles from Chrysler dealer J. A. Edwards that had been hired to advertise Columbia Theater's forthcoming film, *Hold Everything*. Today some homes have been converted to apartments.

Knapp photographed accidents, being around when cars got stuck in the mud, collided, tires went flat, and even when one automobile lost its brakes on the hill at the east end of Church Street. Friends (slightly blurred) apparently are coming to the rescue of the unlucky driver. The home of Penelope Kennedy, granddaughter of county historian William J. McKnight, is in the upper left of the image. The brakes of photographer Clapie's friend worked for the staged image.

Dr. Walter and Mary Geist Dick built their brick California mission-style home in 1929. An athlete, veteran, and community-minded man, Dr. Dick died in 1951. His estate funded the creation of the Walter Dick Memorial Park along the North Fork. After the 1996 flood devastated the area, his family established a perpetual care fund for the park. Today their home and well-landscaped property at 355 Church Street remain a private residence.

Capt. Evans R. Brady fell at the Battle of South Mountain. In 1885, George T. Rodgers bought the home of Brady's widow from Methodist trustees and moved it from the lot just south of its present location. The George T. Rodgers Post No. 102 of the American Legion was chartered in 1919, and members bought Rodgers's home in 1927 for their meeting place. Today it is the home of teachers Chris and Kristie Taylor and their son, Rees Henry.

The Woman's Relief Corps, the auxiliary of the Grand Army of the Republic, established the Pennsylvania Memorial Home in 1890 for Civil War veterans and their dependents in what had been the Hotel Longview on Western Avenue. Today the original brick building and several additions make up the Brookville Borough Complex and Brookville Behavioral Health, Inc. The Woman's Relief Corps has evolved into the WRC that operates the large facility south of the hospital known as Laurelbrook.

As Civil War veterans and their dependents died, World War I veterans and their dependents took their places. Fifteen residents lived in the Pennsylvania Memorial Home when fire struck in 1934. Later, when a memorial to the 10 women who died was dedicated, the Veterans of Foreign Wars Band played. To the center and right are homes that still line Western Avenue. The buildings on the left are part of the Brookville Borough Complex.

Once called the "county poor farm," the Jefferson County Home on State Route 28 north of Brookville was typically home to about 200 indigents annually between 1901 and 1977. Replaced by the new and nearby Jefferson Manor, the old building was renamed the Jefferson County Service Center and housed county offices until 1997. Sold to the Winner Corporation, the building was razed in 2001. Today the county jail, emergency management, and other offices are located on some of the original 200 acres.

A new 28-bed hospital serving more than 40,000 people in Jefferson, Clarion, and Forest Counties opened in 1919. It replaced Dr. Wayne Snyder's small hospital on Franklin Avenue. An adjacent nurses' home was completed in 1928. Additions to the hospital were made in 1950 and 1965. The original hospital building was razed in 1982 and replaced by the current building. Today nearby Clarion and Punxsutawney both have hospitals, and Brookville Hospital is part of the DuBois Regional Medical Center.

CHAPTER 4

Churches, Schools, and Bridges

The Richardsonian Romanesque church that has dominated the corner of Main and White Streets since 1905 is the third house of worship for Brookville Presbyterians. Based upon the Akron Plan popular in 1900, the exterior is constructed of deep red-colored sandstone quarried near Harrisburg, and the roof is a striking green tile. The early duplex on the left was rented.

Presbyterian clergy lived in a variety of homes prior to the completion in 1884 of the French Second Empire manse on property north of the church at a cost of $7,927. When bachelor and wealthy lumberman Paul Darling died in 1881, his will stipulated substantial funds to both individuals and organizations in Brookville. His legacy to the Presbyterian congregation made the manse possible. Both church building and manse are listed on the National Register of Historic Places.

Methodists have worshipped in many buildings: first a barn in 1828, then, like other congregations, in homes, the jail, and the new courthouse. They constructed a building on Jefferson Street in 1852, and when it burned, replaced it with a brick one and selling it to the United Presbyterians while building anew at 130 Pickering Street. Finally, in 1911, they constructed a larger building of Bedford limestone. It burned in 1921, was quickly rebuilt, and is used today.

Dedicated in 1923 as the First Methodist Episcopal Church, the sanctuary, balconies, choir loft, and adjacent areas can accommodate a large number of worshippers. Relatively unchanged, the room is enhanced with arches, chandeliers, amber-tinted art glass windows, dome, quarter-sawed oak flooring, and quarter-sawed oak pews of Gothic design. The original old ivory ceiling and mottled buff walls of the original sanctuary are only slightly modified today.

Methodist circuit riders arrived in 1822 and visited congregations in the south and north of the county. The current parsonage, erected in 1905, is a typical Colonial Revival with a porch on two sides, wide steps, and a large dormer with double windows on the third floor. A succession of clergy—beginning with the Reverend W. P. Graham to the present minister, the Reverend "Mick" Chittester—has lived there with their families.

Between 1831 and 1853, Roman Catholics worshipped in the Peace and Poverty hostelry situated on the northeast corner of Main and Barnett Streets and run by John Dougherty. He gave the land for the first church building that was dedicated in 1853. Worshippers celebrated Mass for the first time in the present church structure on December 8, 1877. Near the church are the rectory and two school buildings that operated between 1869 and 1982.

The first Episcopalians in the county formed the Church of the Intercessor at Sugar Hill around 1850 and established missions in Brookville and Reynoldsville. Brookville Episcopalians worshipped in the Presbyterian and Lutheran churches until 1888, when they constructed this building, copied after a church in Brady's Bend, for $2,250. For three years, the congregation leased the Hotel Longview and operated the Female Episcopal Academy. The double-manual pipe organ installed in 1904 and carillon installed in 1966 are still heard today.

The Free Methodist Church originated in New York in 1860, and the first congregation in Jefferson County formed in Brockwayville in 1894. In Brookville, a congregation erected a crude tabernacle on Church Street in 1895 and replaced it in 1920. The congregation built a dining hall and dormitory in 1952–1953 and remodeled and dedicated the sanctuary, vestibule, and basement in 1978. Today many denominations have church buildings in and around Brookville.

Once students climbed the hill to "Knowledge Knob," where they began first grade and graduated 8 or 12 years later. Brookville's Central School was built in 1878 at a cost of $20,574, and the first high school class graduated in 1886. The estate of Paul Darling, a bachelor and community benefactor, provided the funds to landscape the school grounds. The building was demolished in 1966 when the new junior-senior high school opened on the new campus north of Interstate 80.

The 1898 Paul Darling Memorial Building and 1929 annex added space for an expanding curriculum and a growing student body. The gym was renamed in 1939 for Andy Hastings, a Brookville graduate who was an exceptional athlete at the University of Pittsburgh. The Paul Darling Memorial Building burned in a spectacular fire in 1975. Today, with the exception of the administration building, the property is landscaped as the Northside Park.

Floats for the Brookville centennial parade of 1930 line up in front of the school district's janitor's cottage. The Central School building, the Paul Darling Auditorium, and the Andy Hastings Gymnasium are to the left. Today only the janitor's cottage remains, serving as the administrative offices of the Brookville Area School District, a district that educates about 1,800 students in four buildings: Northside, Pinecreek, and Hickory Grove Elementary Schools and Brookville Area Junior-Senior High School.

In rural areas, vocational and agricultural education became important around the start of the 20th century. Funded by the township and borough school officials, the people of Corsica, a small municipality west of Brookville, dedicated the new Union Vocational School on November 3, 1922. Located on a 4-acre plot, the property included a model home economics house, stables, a small school orchard, and an athletic field. Today the Corsica Volunteer Fire Department is housed in the former school building.

The National Trust for Historic Preservation selected Brookville's Northside School as its poster child in 2001. Completed in 1939 as a Works Progress Administration project of the Roosevelt administration, the exterior of the rectangular redbrick building retains the multi-paned windows, pediments, temple-like entrance, fanlights, and simple detailing of the Colonial Revival style. Dormers dot the gabled roof. The interior, however, has been adapted to the educational needs of today's elementary students.

Commonly called Blake's Bridge due to its location near the former hardware store, the original Waddell A truss bridge was replaced by a Pratt truss bridge before the concrete bridge replaced it in 1926. Eventually the north side of the concrete bridge was replaced, and now plans for a new bridge are underway. The Heber Hotel was razed, and Blake's Buy By the Bridge Hardware (left) that burned in 1994 has been replaced by Ace Hardware.

In 1936, The *Jeffersonian Democrat* reported that the Pennsylvania Highway Department proposed moving the Brookville White Street Bridge "to the location of the Mabon Street bridge over Sandy, and building a new concrete and steel structure at White Street." Finally, in 1941, the metal girders and wooden sidewalk of a new pony truss bridge connected both sides of the Red Bank Creek at White Street and eliminated two bad curves of the previous roadway. The truss bridge was replaced in 1995.

John Cook surveyed the Clarion River area in 1826, and then he built a homestead and mill. Descendents preserved a large section of virgin timber, and in 1928 they and the Commonwealth of Pennsylvania designated 7,219 acres as Cook Forest State Park, the state's first effort to preserve a natural landmark. The Forest Cathedral became a National Natural Landmark in 1969. Historic Brookville lies just south of and is a gateway to this appropriate symbol of Pennsylvania's lumber heritage.

For nearly half a century, Frederick E. Knapp documented places and events around Brookville and took studio portraits of prominent men and beautiful women, soldiers of two world wars, young boys and their first deer, young girls and their dance cards, children with their toys, and babies on blankets. He also had a wonderful sense of humor, as illustrated by his bearded self-portrait, a stark contrast to the more formal portrait taken mid-career. His work is a lasting legacy.

www.arcadiapublishing.com